TINY TRUMPETS

TINY TRUMPETS:
REFLECTIONS ON LIFE & GOD & GRACE

LALOR CADLEY

Tiny Trumpets: Reflections on Life & God & Grace

Reflections 3, 7, and 12 are revised versions of columns
published in the Atlanta Journal Constitution.
Reflection 15 was first published in Richard Rohr's *Radical Grace*.

Each reflection is accompanied by an image.
These images were purchased from on-line sources –
Shutterstock, Dreamstime, or iStock Photo – unless otherwise noted.

Composition of cover photo by Nan Ross
Cover art and book design by Laura Nalesnik at MouseWhiskers Studio
MouseWhiskers.com
Layout and design by Felicia Kahn
Hibiscus blossom design element by Peter Lalor Ferrari
Author Photo by Oliver Daniel Ferrari

ISBN: 978-0-692-38761-0

DEDICATION

To my grandfather
who taught me the art of cherishing

CONTENTS

Welcome!

When I was young I used to love Advent, that special time of year set aside by the Church to prepare for the coming of Christ on Christmas Day. I especially loved those magical Advent calendars with the little numbered doors. Each morning before breakfast one of us children would get to break open the door for that day, and behind it would be an angel, a star, perhaps a tiny trumpet. Each day moved us one step closer to Christmas and the birth of Jesus.

I'd like to offer these fifteen reflections as little doorways, openings onto the mystery of the God who is with us still, as present to us now in Spirit as He was embodied in Jesus two thousand years ago. Unlike the Advent calendar, they don't have to be opened in order, but each is meant to offer a way to recognize and celebrate the nearness and dearness of God, and the wonder of this holy world in which we live and move and have our being.

I am especially eager that the book be available to those who, like me, were raised with the idea that God – though a benevolent being, to be sure – was somewhat remote, unapproachable except when all else failed. More king than shepherd, mighty and majestic, receiver of prayers, forgiver of sin. Our task as faithful followers was to obey Him, to serve Him in this world and be happy with Him in the next.

It wasn't until I was in my 40's, when I returned to school to be trained in spiritual direction, that I was exposed to a whole new face of God. This "new" God was not remote, isolated, looking down from on high. This God was here and now, deeply relational, closer to us than our breath, alive in every moment of our lives. The greatest desire of this God was not to be served but to be known and loved.

How it happened, this welcome evolution in my understanding, I can't say exactly. It had to do with reading lots of good contemporary theologians' work, having enlightened spiritual directors to guide me. It also had to do with listening to people who came to my office month in and month out, people committed to leading a life in tune with the Spirit; and seeing how God loved them to life. Watching their lives unfurl – as they learned to listen for Her movement and respond to Her call – I came to know a God who loves us dearly just as we are, who never holds our trespasses against us, and who is tirelessly working to heal our wounds and bring us to life. This God longs for us, delights in us, listens for the sound of our voice, is eager to live in us and through us.

It's true. The God whose presence we seek during formal prayer times or in Church on Sunday mornings, is also present when we read books or feed birds or drive cars or make love. Our daily lives are an ongoing source of revelation, the ground on which the Spirit sings Her song of love. We need only have ears to hear and eyes to see.

Over the years, watching people's lives transform as they became more attentive and responsive to this simple, hidden melody, I have come to believe that our primary work as faithful people is to wake up to this daily life we live, to see it as another kind of Scripture. Listening must become the cornerstone of our lives. And as we listen to our lives, we learn God's ways; we sense that we are being called to open to God's longing and give way to God's dream for our lives.

Our willingness is everything. Our Yes brings God to life.

My prayer is that, in sharing these stories from my own life, I will have helped you see more clearly the ways God moves in you – comforting you, challenging you, guiding you, bringing you to fullness of life in Her image.

Of these fifteen pieces, some are about moments of grace in the midst of creation, times when the veil was lifted and the Hidden One shone through. Others are about dark times, when the experience was one of anguish and abandonment, and only after hard struggle could Love be found at the heart of the pain. You'll find reflections on some of my favorite women in Scripture. A piece on the ambiguous place of suffering in the life of good Christians. There is a reflection on prayer – prayer not as an activity we engage in but as a way of life rooted in relationship.

More than one of the pieces speaks about the art of listening deeply – not just to others but to our selves, and to the God of our life. I have included a reflection on the important subject of God language, and freely share my frustration with the current state of things. In another piece I tell about an encounter with a man in a lavender shirt on a Provincetown dock that gave new urgency to my ministry. You will find reflections on my dear dog Jessie and my beloved "grandad," both shining ambassadors of God's amazing grace.

As I read over the pieces one more time, preparing to release them into the air, my hope is that at the very least they will help to lighten your load, illumine your path, and strengthen your faith in the beauty of Love's way.

Author's Note
with regard to the use of pronouns for God

As you see, I have used both male and female pronouns
when referring to the Divine. This practice helps me remember
that God is neither "He" nor "She" but pure Spirit.
Using feminine pronouns also gives me easier access
to God's tenderness and quiet love, as a counterweight
to God's might and majesty.

1

AN ARDENT APPARITION

*"Be who God meant you to be,
and you will set the world on fire."*

~ Catherine of Siena

There are times when life gets so crammed, so speedy, so senseless that I think if I don't get off the wheel I will shatter into a thousand pieces. I fly through my days getting from one thing to the next, never being where I am because there is always somewhere else to go. It's as if life has turned into a video game: the more bases I tag before time runs out, the more points I score.

Now this is no way to live, and we know it. It's bad for our health, our work, our family life. It keeps us distracted, irritable, prone to migraines and fender benders. But the worst of it is, in the rush of it all, we miss our lives.

Sometimes the only way to restore myself to sanity is to take myself away. I go off for two or three days to a quiet place, steeped in prayer, where God can have my full attention and I can be rebalanced. The frequency of these getaways depends on how desperate I get and how willing I am to do something about it. I try to go at least three times a year.

It is an experience I had on one of those retreats that I want to share with you. It was an experience that testifies to the nearness and dearness of God, and what this God can do when we are willing to stop spinning and show up fully present Here and Now. It also makes clear what we may miss if we don't.

The incident took place at a spirituality center in Houston where I had gone for a three-day retreat. The retreat was being conducted by a Cenacle Sister who had been my spiritual director for years, a woman widely known for her quiet love of life and God. Under her unassuming guidance, I had been working to dislodge a longstanding image of God as distant and demanding – expecting more of me than I was able to deliver.

In our monthly sessions she had been challenging me to open to a new experience of God, an experience of God as love, only love; as One who delights in me just as I am and wants to share life with me. I remember coming home from one of our sessions and writing on a Post-it note that I stuck to the bathroom mirror: "What if God isn't measuring me but enjoying me?"

After a morning of talks on the spiritual life and a satisfying lunch, Sister gave us an optional afternoon activity. We were invited to wander the grounds of the retreat center until we came upon an object in nature that drew our attention. When we found something that called to us, we were to approach the object, still ourselves, and listen for what the object might have to say to us. Then we were free to offer a response.

"Go off now," she said. "Take your journals with you. All you have to do is open your eyes, open your hearts, and let it come." Sister never doubted that if we would take time for God, God would be there for us.

I waited until the room was nearly empty, fighting a curious temptation to avoid the exercise. Doubts rose up and tumbled around in my head. What if nothing happened? What if I picked the wrong object? What if I missed the thing that was meant for me, or misinterpreted its meaning? Maybe I did need to go back to my room and take a nap after all.

Finally I made my choice. I gathered up my journal, settled my sweater over my shoulders, and headed out the back door onto the patio, thinking I might walk down to the bayou. I looked down to check the suitability of my shoes – the path is often muddy near the water – and when I looked up it was as if the whole world had been washed in a golden light. The grass, the trees, the sky were luminous, pulsing with life.

I closed my eyes and took a deep breath. I must have said a prayer, though truthfully I can't remember. I do remember that when I opened my eyes I saw before me a huge hibiscus plant, laden with lush red flowers the size of saucers. A living thing, ablaze with glory. From the center of each velvet flower bright yellow tendrils quivered, like tiny trumpets sounding silent praise. I leaned in to get a closer look, and was hit with the absolute, unmistakable awareness that God was in this place. I was standing on holy ground. There was no audible voice, no vision, just a clear, bright knowing that God was showing.

Just then a gentle breeze set the flowers swaying and I felt myself being drawn deeper in – summoned, you might say, to open to this ardent apparition. This God who for so long had been lodged in my mind as taskmaster/scorekeeper/ judge, peering down from on high with a rule book in hand, came to me now garbed in lush red velvet, winking and waving, singing and swaying, all fragrance and music and lighthearted laughter.

I watched transfixed, barely breathing for fear it might all go away. After a while I heard these words in my head: "You too are meant to bloom and blaze."

I dropped down on a nearby bench, closed my eyes, and prayed, "Help me know that this is You; help me believe that this is true."

The vision was over in an instant, but in that instant a latch had been lifted in me. The God of my life, so long confined behind walls of oughts and shoulds, was set free. I was opened to a God who comes as lover, life-giver, dearest of friends. This was a God to whom I could surrender, a God to whom I would gladly give my consent.

When I came home and got back to my day-to-day life, the wonder faded. But I never lost the treasure God had given. That was mine to keep.

So the next time you feel overwhelmed and undernourished, not knowing where you are or where you're going, perhaps you could see this as an invitation to come away and rest awhile, to put yourself in the hands of the God of your life, and see what She has for you. Who knows what gift might await you, what burning bush may call your name?

Reflection Questions:

- Have you ever had a "burning bush" experience?

- What is your image of God?
  Has it changed over the years?
  How has it influenced you?

- What do you need to live more fully, more freely,
  more joyfully?

Journal

_____

_____

_____

_____

_____

_____

_____

_____

_____

_____

_____

_____

_____

_____

_____

_____

_____

_____

_____

_____

_____

_____

_____

_____

Journal

_____
_____
_____
_____
_____
_____
_____
_____
_____
_____
_____
_____
_____
_____
_____
_____
_____
_____
_____
_____
_____
_____
_____
_____
_____
_____
_____

2

GRANDAD

"Love one another as I have loved you."
~ John 13:34

I had the most wonderful grandfather. I wish everyone could have had someone like him in their lives. He loved me in a way I've not been loved before or since. He loved me not because I was smart or pretty or talented or entertaining. He loved me simply because I was.

From the moment I was born we were a pair. The year was 1943. My parents had separated during my mother's pregnancy. My father was in the army, stationed in Dayton, Ohio. My mother had moved back to Brooklyn to live with her parents. It was not a happy time for her. Much as she wanted to want me, it was clear she would have preferred to be unencumbered. Grandad, perhaps sensing her ambivalence, took on the task of raising me. Lucky girl!

After the war my parents got back together again and rented an apartment in Brooklyn, within walking distance of my grandparents. Visits were regular and frequent. Then when I was five, we moved to Long Island, to a house that would accommodate a growing family. But every Sunday after Mass we'd drive back to Brooklyn to share Sunday dinner with Granny and Grandad – roast leg of lamb with kelly green jelly, buttery potatoes, soggy green beans, and for dessert Breyer's vanilla ice cream with homemade chocolate sauce.

While we waited to be called to dinner, I would climb into my Grandad's lap and he would draw for me. He had two drawings in his repertoire: the spread wings of a seagull in flight and the backside of a bulldog. The bulldog's backside got my Grandma fussing but it made me laugh. Over and over he would draw the same two things, and I would watch, and now and then he'd pass the pencil on to me and I would do some of my own.

Once dinner was over, the dishes washed and put away, I would look to him and he would wink. That was our signal to get our coats from the closet and head out for our afternoon walk – he in his tweed suit, starched white shirt and tie, in winter a grey wool overcoat, always a hat with a brim; I in my pale pink coat with the fur collar and covered buttons, a matching hat and patent leather shoes with ankle straps.

Brooklyn in those days was charming – streets lined with beautiful old four-story brownstones, mahogany doors with shiny brass knockers, well-tended gardens bordered by ornate wrought iron fences, every few feet a tall shade tree planted in a patch of soil cut from the concrete. On Sunday afternoons the sidewalks were filled with people strolling to and fro – young couples, old people, dogs, and children.

We'd walk along, his hand holding mine, his stride just matching mine. No need to hurry, no place to go. It was up to me to decide when we'd walked far enough and were ready to rest. I'd pick out a stoop, and draw him to it. "Let's sit," I'd say, "and have a conversation."

We'd settle ourselves close together on the concrete stoop, his tweed trouser leg rough against my bare shin. I'd wait as he pulled out of his breast pocket a black enamel cigar case, snapped it open and took out a cigar stub, which he'd put in his mouth, unlit. Grandma had made him give up smoking long ago, but this proximate pleasure was apparently still allowed. The only other time the stub came out was during chess games.

He adored chess, my Grandad. And he was good at it. Rumor had it he'd been one of Bobby Fischer's early teachers. He kept a chess board under the double windows in the small living room of their ground floor flat and used to play every day against himself. When he was pondering a move he'd twirl that cigar round and round. Then, when he had decided what to do, he'd stick the stub in his mouth and reach for the piece, hovering over the chosen space until he was sure it was the best move he could make. For hours he'd walk from one side of the board to the other, twirling his cigar stub, making moves and counter moves, until one side or the other "won." Then he'd return the pieces to their starting places and start all over again.

When we were comfortably settled on the stoop, I'd begin. I would tell him everything that was on my mind – about school, about my friends, about the annoying thing my little brother had done, about what I hoped to get for my birthday. He would sit quietly, attentively, looking at the ground and chewing on the tip of his cigar.

When the sun began to set and the stone on which we sat made our bottoms cold, he would signal that the time had come for us to make our way back home. My Dad didn't like to leave the city later than 5:00. He said we needed time to get ready for the week ahead.

It always made me a little sad, getting up and going back. One time (so the story goes) I was so determined to stay put, my Grandad had to call the Irish cop on the corner to come over and put his weight behind Grandad's request. "Ok, little girl, it's time to move along," he said, twirling his billy club. "It's getting late, and the people who live here will be coming home soon." All the while he spoke, he and Grandad exchanged broad grins.

There is one thing more about my Grandad I haven't mentioned. He was stone deaf. Rheumatic fever had destroyed his hearing when he was 16. He did have a hearing aid but he seldom wore it except at work.

And so, for all those long and lively "conversations,"when we talked about my life, my cares, my hopes and dreams, he never heard a word. And it didn't matter. It was his presence, so loving and still, that was his offering. And it was all I needed to open up and pour myself out. Years later, talking about him with my spiritual director, she said, "Sounds like you had the perfect channel – love. Words weren't necessary; they might even have gotten in the way."

He died when I was thirteen. At his funeral so many people spoke about what a good man he was. They talked about the strength of his faith. (He had great devotion to Mary and used to say the rosary daily, attributing miracles to her intercession.) About his love for his family, especially his wife, "My Mary." (Apparently he used to leave love notes for her around the house, hidden under lamps or tucked into a shoe.) About his bedrock integrity.

He had worked as a civil engineer, and was widely known for his honesty in an era of rampant corruption. I remember mother telling us how he would rise before dawn to be on site when the concrete was poured for the sewer lines, to be sure corners weren't being cut to increase profits.

My favorite story was one told by his nurse, a self-proclaimed agnostic and the only one in the room when he died: "It was so beautiful," she said. "Just before he went, he raised his arms and smiled. Someone came for him."

To this day, when life with all its expectations and demands threatens my peace of mind, I find myself remembering back to those days, sitting in grandad's lap. Smelling his cologne, laced with the faint aroma of tobacco, feeling the scratchy wool of his tweed suit against my leg, watching him draw me seagulls' wings and bulldogs' behinds, until I am calm and can go back out again.

How I wish everyone had had a grandfather like mine. I'll bet the world would be a very different place if the people who make such terrible trouble had known that kind of love when they were young. It is a saving love, a mirror of God's love. Surely that kind of love could heal the wounds that make us wicked, and bring the world to peace. In fact, isn't it the only thing that ever will?

Reflection Questions:

• What is your experience of unconditional love?

• How did your grandparents influence your sense of self and God?

• Is there a place in your life where you can speak your deepest truths and be heard?

Journal

Ric Fallis

3

JESSIE LOVE

"...in all that they do, they give life."
~ Nan Merrill, *Psalms for Praying*

Her name was Jessie – Jessica officially, but we only called her that when she crossed the line. She was our dog for fifteen years, our beagle/dachshund, with just enough retriever so she couldn't meet us at the door without something in her mouth – a stray sock, a scrap of paper, whatever she could get to in a hurry.

We'd walk in and there she'd be, velvet ears perked, brown eyes wide, back end swinging to and fro like windshield wipers in a rainstorm. It didn't matter how long we'd been gone – an hour, a day, or a week; her welcome was always Five Star.

We'd gotten her as a pup, from the Atlanta Humane Society. She was a perfect dog for us, lively and loving, quick to accommodate to the ups and downs of our lickety split lives.

Just after her fifteenth birthday, we began to notice troubling signs of aging in her. Her eyesight began to fade; her arthritis got worse; the treats that used to make her prance and twirl lay forgotten on the ground. Even when we tried to coax her to play – one practice that had never failed was to gather round the island in the kitchen and clap-clap-clap madly, while she raced from room to room, skidding round the corners, flipping up the rugs, sending our poor cats into orbit – even when we'd clap for her, she'd only glance up from her bed then turn away.

Going for walks became an ordeal. Getting her to rise up out of bed was painful. She couldn't rely on her back legs to hold her up. She'd get going, then collapse onto her bottom, looking bewildered and vaguely embarrassed. The vet increased her pain medication, which helped some, but only for a while.

Weeks went by. I kept her close. Then one early morning, sitting on the floor of my bedroom with her head in my lap, I asked the question into the quiet, and the answer came: it's time. I approached the boys, both in their late teens at the time. Each took a different position, one maintaining that it wasn't right to put her down, the other insisting that it wasn't fair not to. I remained on the sidelines, admiring their willingness to struggle until the way became clear. At one point I even found myself wondering if they might have to have a similar conversation around my bedside someday.

"It's not just the quantity of life that counts, but the quality," said the younger one. "Look at her – she can't see, she can't hear, she can barely walk! Most days she just sleeps or stares into space. How do we know she's not in pain? I think it's time."

"But what if she's not ready?" his brother responded. "What if we are making this decision for us and not for her, because we're tired of cleaning up after her, or because we can't stand to see her like this? We've got to be sure we're doing it because it's right for her, not just convenient for us."

While they debated, Jessie's decline started to accelerate. It was almost as if she understood our dilemma. One day it just came clear to all of us that this dear dog who'd lit up our lives for so many years, who'd made the good times better and helped us weather the bad, was asking us to let her go.

We called the vet that day to discuss options. She told us we could bring Jessie to her clinic, or we could have the procedure done at home, which was more costly but would make it easier on Jessie – and on us.

The vet arrived next morning at 11:00. Jessie was lying in her bed with us around her on the floor. The vet shaved a small patch on her lower leg, inserted a needle through a frail vein and began administering the drugs. All the while, we stroked her head and spoke her name.

After a while she simply stopped breathing. The vet checked her heart, assured us she was gone, and left. We wrapped her in a cotton blanket, took her to a wooded area where a small grave had been dug, eased her gently into the ground, sprinkled water and flower petals over her body, and said a short prayer. It was a prayer of gratitude and the last line rang like bells: "...in all that they do, they give life."

Afterwards, we returned to the house, sat together for a while in the quiet, then shared lunch, our signature special-occasion lunch – cheese tortellini with homemade meat sauce. All in all, it was a good day, a sad day but a good day. Even in death she gave us life.

Reflection Questions:

- How have animals touched your life?

- Have you ever had to decide how to help end the life of another living being?

- What brings life and love to you these days?

Journal

4

THE MAN ON THE DOCK

"...they desire a better homeland."
~ Hebrews 11

Sitting by the window of my sister's condo in Province-town, looking out on the quiet Sunday morning street below, my journal open on my lap, I sip coffee – Starbucks French Roast – and recall a conversation from the night before with a man on a dock, a conversation that keeps tugging on me like a child in need of attention.

I take up my pen to write – writing helps me sort things out – then put it down again. I lean back and close my eyes. Immediately I am flooded with scenes from the night before. I am back on the dock.

It is a glorious evening, the lavender sky awash with streaks of bright peach, casting a film of chiffon light across the water. The dock is crowded with people, men and women; some are friends of my sister. Talk is of trips they've taken, places they are planning to go; the whereabouts of mutual friends; kitchen renovations that aren't going well; the new chef in town whose bouillabaisse is worth the wait.

At one point I find myself standing next to a man impeccably dressed in white trousers and a starched lavender shirt. We get to talking and he tells me he recently retired from a New York law firm and spends most of his time traveling. When he asks what I do, I feel inside a familiar twinge. Telling someone you're a spiritual director can stop a conversation dead in its tracks. People just want to get away. Either that or they want you to read their palm.

Which is why I was pleasantly surprised when the man greeted my announcement with a genuine show of interest. "Tell me more," he said.

Within minutes I find myself telling him about the people I serve, people seeking lives of meaning and purpose, lives that reflect their values and give substance to their faith. "We all want lives that are true to who we are, don't you think?" He nods. "We want lives that give us happiness and joy." And how do we get from here to there? I hesitate, then decide to take my chances. "For me, and for the people I journey with, it begins by putting ourselves in the hands of the God who made us and knows us and wants us to have a full and fruitful life." I tell him how much of my work is convincing people to trust God's will for them; helping them heal from religious abuse and come to know both God's great kindness and their own essential goodness.

The man is leaning in now. His partner has strolled over and is standing on the outskirts of our conversation. "When do people come to you?" he asks.

"They come at different times, and for various reasons. Often they come when the things that used to satisfy don't have the same appeal anymore, and they wonder where to go from here." The silence that follows is broken by a knowing laugh. These are men in their 60s, wealthy, well established, nearing the time when life inevitably shifts into a lower gear and that disquieting question, "What's it all about?" begins to rise up. Judging from the sound of their laugh, I guess neither is a stranger to this discontent. What they don't know is that it is divine, God's way of calling them home.

He shakes his head, then hands the waiter his empty glass and orders another dry martini. I remain silent; it is up to him whether we end the conversation here or move to the next level.

"The God I grew up with was a tyrant," he says after a while. "You obeyed the rules or risked damnation. Of course being gay I was pretty well damned from the get go." He shrugs, then looks around for the waiter to bring him his drink.

Just then the maître'd calls my sister's name. Our table is ready. I thank him for the conversation. He nods then turns to join another group. I follow my sister and her friends to our table, my head swimming with what I have just been given. For him our conversation may be over; for me it has just begun.

I take up my pen and this time there is no doubt that I'm ready. Words fly onto the page as if they have been waiting a long time for an opening.

It has become clear to me over twenty years in this ministry of spiritual direction that too many good people have given up on religion, and for good reason. Take this man I met last night, a gay man, raised in a religious tradition that taught him homosexuals were a shame to their families and a sinner in the eyes of God. What choice did he have? He could lie or he could leave. So he left. To stay would have cost him his soul.

I put down my pen and think of all the thousands like him, men and women who have left the Church because they felt unwelcome, good people whose trust had been betrayed. My beloved sister is among them.

I remember the day she told me she had cut her ties with the Church. It was right after she came out to my parents at eighteen. She knew they loved her dearly, and that would never change. She had no fear they would reject her; her fear was that the Church's rejection of her would cause them great heartache. As devout Roman Catholics, they were raised to believe that the Pope was Christ's Vicar on earth and papal teachings came down from on high. To challenge the Church was tantamount to challenging Christ. And the Church's teachings on the subject of homosexuality were loud and clear: homosexuality was a disorder; practicing homosexuals were living in sin and endangering their immortal souls.

This left my parents in a terrible bind, one my father never did resolve entirely. Until the end he lived with the faint fear that my sister's "choice" might have jeopardized her salvation. Fortunately my mother was able to make a dent in his worry by reminding him regularly that the God she knew would never turn anyone away.

How a Church charged with the sacred responsibility of bringing Christ to life in the world could have done this – pitting good parents against their own children – is beyond belief. Not to mention that a sizable percentage of dedicated religious men and women are homosexual. What must it be like for them, giving their lives to an institution that refuses to accept them in the fullness of their humanity.

As I said, the cost to my parents was high. The cost to my sister was high as well. Walking away was not easy for her, though I didn't know this until years later. It was during a visit to her in Boston. I had come for the weekend and was planning to attend Sunday Mass at the Paulist Center, a liberal Catholic community that had been home to me when I lived in Boston years before. On a whim I invited her to join me, "for old time's sake." To my surprise, she agreed.

The service was simple; the sermon was sound; the community included a sizable number of gays and lesbians, men and women who moved comfortably in the space. After the service, I invited her to join me in line to greet the priest. She signaled that she'd rather not, and headed out the door. When I joined her minutes later on the sidewalk, I turned her toward me to give her a hug and saw that she had been crying. Her cheeks were wet with tears.

I pick up my pen and continue:

O how I would love to have a special ministry to those who've given up. I would like to find them all, and bring them to my office and plump up the cushions and pour cups of tea and sit them down and let them talk, and I would simply listen. And when they were finished, and I was sure they had no more to say, I would affirm their choice.

Then I would pose a question, a gentle wondering. Was it possible that, in leaving the Church, they had left behind a treasure hidden in the field? Perhaps God, the One True God who made them and loved them, was waiting to be rescued from the refuse bin, untangled from those toxic teachings that were not God's truth but man's misunderstandings, stamped with the seal of a god made in their image?

What if God was utterly opposed to the habit of religious institutions to label, judge, exclude, condemn? What if the refusal of these so-called "unbelievers" to buy into it was not an indication of infidelity but a holy resistance prompted by the very God they'd been accused of abandoning?

I pause, check my watch – still half an hour before I have to rise up and get ready for Sunday services at the little Episcopal Church down the road. My sister and her partner have gone off to play golf. We'll meet in town for brunch at noon.

As I said, I don't for one minute lament their rejection of religion. This ache in me comes from a fear that, in turning their back on religion, they may lose touch with the living God. God remains trapped inside the walls of the institution, tarred with the same brush. And that hunger for God that is at the core of every human being, a hunger that only God can satisfy, seeks satisfaction elsewhere – in cars and clothes and cocktails and prime real estate.

Once God is no longer in the picture, we leave ourselves wide open to a culture hawking counterfeit satisfactions night and day, a culture lavishly supported by people whose access to God has been cut off and whose appetite for God has nowhere else to go.

If I were starting a religion now I would start with the people and not with the rules. Like Jesus did. I would call Zacchaeus out of the tree and invite myself to his home for dinner. I would bring wine and bread and a heart wide open to his story. I would pray for God to create between us a space safe enough for him to speak. And as he spoke I would recognize his yearnings – for love, for life. I would ask him to come again and bring his friends, and slowly trust would build and he might be persuaded to give God another chance.

We might have to burn some books, reject traditional teachings, create new rituals designed to open us to joy. We'd need to place compassion back in first place, give opportunities for penitence that took us safely around the swampland of shame and led us into God's embrace where we could be truly sorry for what truly are our sins. Never ever would we have to be sorry for being who we are.

Maybe if there were a church like that, the man on the dock would be tempted to give it a try. Or not. What matters isn't whether people find their way back to Church but whether people who have given up on Church find their way back to God. Many, to be sure, have found God in other places, but this man whom I was given saw God and Church as inextricably bound. His Church's betrayal had cost him his God. And that's a price no one should have to pay.

I have no more to say now. It's almost time for Services. My prayer going forward is that this encounter will not have been in vain. That I will be given the grace to hear the cries of those who want to be found, and can create a space where they can feel safe to open their hearts to the God of Love who waits to welcome them home.

Reflection Questions:

- How does this story speak to you in your own life?

- Have you ever felt a dissonance between Church teachings and your inner knowing?

- What is the desire of your heart for people who can't find a home in the tradition?

Journal

_____

_____

_____

_____

_____

_____

_____

_____

_____

_____

_____

_____

_____

_____

_____

_____

_____

_____

_____

_____

_____

_____

_____

Journal

5

WOMAN AT THE WELL

One of the many things I love about Jesus was the way he supported, protected, encouraged and enjoyed women. As we know, women weren't highly thought of in those days, to say the least, and yet Jesus seems to go out of his way again and again to raise them up and send them forth.

Examples abound. In the story of Mary and Martha, for example, he defends Mary's right to step out of the kitchen and into the conversation. It would seem from what he says – "Mary has chosen the better part, and it will not be taken from her" – that her presence there beside him means more to him than any service she might provide. (Luke 10:38-42)

In the story of the woman caught in adultery, he steps between a defenseless woman and an angry mob of men carrying stones, and shames them into submission by turning the tables with one swift brilliant move: "Let the one among you who is without sin cast the first stone." (John 8:3-11)

In the story of the woman who enters the house of Simon the Leper uninvited and pours precious oil over Jesus' head, he silences the protesters and celebrates the woman. "She has done a beautiful thing to me." (Matt 26:6-13)

At the resurrection it is to Mary Magdalene – not Peter, James or John – that Jesus chooses to appear. It is to her that he gives the responsibility of spreading the news. (John 20:11-18)

The list goes on.

(I have often wondered if one of the reasons Jesus could see so clearly the beauty and worth of women was because he was raised by a woman whose wisdom, courage, and faithful love permeated his being from the day he was born.)

One of my favorite examples of his love and care for women comes in the Gospel of John (John 4:1-30; 39-42). It is the story of Jesus and the Samaritan woman at the well, and it is on this story that I would like to focus my reflection. When I first heard this Scripture, back in my Catholic school days, I read it as a nice story about Jesus being kind to a woman no one liked, a woman with a "past." He talks with her, forgives her sins, and sends her on her way. It was one among many stories in the Gospels in which Jesus heals and saves.

It wasn't until I went back to graduate school in the early 90's that the story began to shine for me. For one thing I learned about the historical context in which the story took place. Without that, we can't fully appreciate how radical Jesus' actions were. It was also during that time that I was in the midst of my own struggle to come into a fuller version of myself, to become more open to God's transforming power in my life.

The story opens with Jesus returning to his hometown of Galilee from Judea where he has been preaching and baptizing. The number of his followers is growing rapidly and the Pharisees are taking notice. Time for him to make himself scarce. The shortest route back to Galilee is through Samaria. And this is the route he chooses, despite the fact that Samaria is seen as enemy territory, and Jews customarily go the long way round to avoid it. Jews despised the Samaritans for condoning practices they deemed anathema – intermarrying with pagans; accepting only the Pentateuch as their Scripture; not recognizing the Temple as the center of worship.

The scene opens with Jesus, "tired out by his journey," sitting by a well. It is noon time. The sun is high and blistering hot. We imagine him sitting on the stone wall, his shoulders slumped perhaps, his feet swollen from countless miles of walking over sand and rock. His back aches, his throat is parched and dry.

He is alone, having sent the disciples into the village to buy food. Enter a woman carrying a bucket, a Samaritan woman. She comes to draw water from this well after the other women have come and gone. Better to bear the blistering heat of the noonday sun than the sting of their scorn.

She is startled by his presence. He is a Jew, for one thing. What is he doing here, sitting alone in the noonday sun? And...Could it be?...Is she imagining it...or does he seem to be waiting for her? We can almost feel the mix of fear and fascination running through her as she stands before him, alert but not budging, not turning away.

He speaks, and what he says is blunt, imperative: "Give me a drink."

Now this is a shocking move on so many levels it's hard to know where to begin. We can almost hear the cultural taboos shattering as they hit the ground. First, he is a man, and men in those times did not speak to strange women in public. Second, he is a Rabbi, and Rabbi's *really* didn't speak to strange women in public. Third, she is a Samaritan, and Jews do not associate with Samaritans. As if that weren't enough, she is not any Samaritan woman but a woman shunned by her own people for her unsavory past. An outcast among outcasts. One would be hard pressed to come up with someone lower down on the pecking order than she is.

His request stuns her. "How is it that you, a Jew, ask a drink of me, a woman of Samaria?"

Now those of us who know God's ways are not surprised by this. We get that something's up; she's being prepared. This God, who is full of surprises, is inviting her to something new. I am reminded of Mary at the Annunciation – a virgin being asked to bear a child. Imagine! It's as if God enjoys poking holes in our cherished assumptions, turning dead ends into bright possibilities.

Jesus responds with a cryptic but compelling invitation: "If only you knew who I was and what I am offering, you would have been the one asking me for a drink, and I would have given you living water."

The woman is caught off balance by this shift from the literal to the metaphorical. What is he talking about? Is he thirsty or not? Is there something more going on here?

She responds with the utmost pragmatism: "Sir, you have no bucket, and the well is deep. Where do you get that living water?"...Pause...(no response). Then, "Jacob gave us this well. He drank here. Are you saying it's not good enough? You've got something better?"

Jesus speaks back to her – patient, kind, alluring. This water is fine, as far as it goes. But it can only give you temporary refreshment. You have to keep coming back every day for more. (This she knows well, and has raw sores on her shoulders to prove it.) The real thirst, the thirst you won't name but I know is in you, is a thirst for love, for acceptance, for belonging. It is a thirst for the Living God. And it is a thirst only I can quench. "The water that I will give will become a spring of water gushing up to eternal life."

This woman whose kinswomen won't give her the time of day is being given a chance to receive the greatest gift on earth, the gift of eternal life. At this point, something shifts inside her. She gets it.

She gets it in a way no one else has, not the crowds he has been preaching to, or the religious authorities he has been running from, not even his own disciples..."***Give me a drink,*** " she says, "so that I may never be thirsty again or have to keep coming here to draw water." She is opening herself. For this woman who has been hurt so many times, this must have been a huge gamble.

Jesus' reply is a surprise. We think he is going to give her the water. Instead he turns the wheel of the story in a whole new direction. "Go call your husband and come back." Before she can receive the new life, she must be unburdened, freed from the guilt and shame of her past. Reconciliation is being offered. But at first she doesn't see it this way.

"Go call your husband and come back?!" It must have felt like a slap in the face.

Her response is forthright, unapologetic. "I have no husband!" This woman is used to defending herself.

Jesus has no wish to embarrass her. His only desire is to free her from the straight-jacket in which her past has imprisoned her, so that God's mercy can flow freely and restore her to life. "That's the truth." he says. "Though you have had five husbands, the one you're with now is not your husband."

Something in the tone of his voice convinces her that she is not being shamed. He is teasing her. This frees her to respond playfully, in keeping with the tone of the interchange: "I see that you are a prophet!" she says. Perhaps they share a laugh.

Then the mood shifts again. A stillness surrounds them as they move to a place of exquisite vulnerability. With Jesus listening attentively, she is able to tell her story, all of it, leaving nothing out.

They go on in the light of the setting sun. The conversation turns to theology. Perhaps now that he has heard her, she wants to learn more about him. Scripture scholars tell us that nowhere – *nowhere* – in all of Scripture do we find an exchange of this length or depth between Jesus and another person. What's remarkable is that the woman can hold her own here too. She asks good questions, and follows where he leads. Surely she is not educated, but somehow she has become informed. Perhaps the men with whom she keeps company like having her around for their discussions. Perhaps in those late nights that went on until dawn she was exposed to issues and ideas more cloistered women missed out on. Who knows? But somehow she was up to this conversation, the fruits of which are being harvested to this day.

Notice that things happen for Jesus as well in this sacred place, this time out of time. It is here that Jesus speaks for the first time about the true nature of God ("God is spirit"). When the woman asks him where God should be worshipped, on the mountain (the Samaritans' position) or in the Temple (the Jews' position), Jesus tells her that what really matters is not where you worship but how you worship.

Then comes the revelation that will change the course of human history. "The hour is coming, and is now here, when true worshippers will worship the Father in spirit and truth." The hour is coming... "Ah," she says: "I know that Messiah is coming who is the Christ. When he comes he will proclaim all things to us."

Here, what I imagine is a long pause, in which Jesus decides whether to break his code of silence and reveal to this woman of Samaria, this outcast, what so many have been wondering since he came on the scene. Will this be the moment, will this be the person to whom he discloses his true identity as the Messiah, the Anointed One of God?

"I am he. I am the one you have been waiting for."

Clearly something very powerful has taken place between them, and it has not been all one way. Just as she has been profoundly re-formed by trusting him with her story, is it possible he too has been changed, confirmed in his own identity, by speaking these words to this woman in this lonely place? "I am he." Has a thirst in Jesus also been satisfied this day?

Our story ends with the arrival of the disciples, who, as is often the case, are clueless, although not one of them has the nerve to ask Jesus, "What are you doing with her?" I guess by now they are used to being stupefied.

The woman takes off, back to the village, radiant with the grace of new life. Her transformation is apparently so breathtaking that people are willing to see her with totally new eyes, to believe what she says and follow where she leads. "Many Samaritans of that town believed in him on the strength of the woman's testimony."

What I treasure most about this story is the mutuality. Not only does Jesus not chastise her for her poor choices; he doesn't patronize her either. He takes seriously her questions, listens well to what she says, embraces her in all her flawed perfection, and anoints her with the priestly work of spreading the good news.

In a Church where women's roles are still circumscribed, it feels good and right and a joyful thing to share a story in which Jesus so clearly trusts, respects, and celebrates a woman, inviting her to become part of his saving work. I think about the woman herself and what she might say to us as we make our way deeper into God and deeper into the world God loves. *God is not who you think God is. And you are not who you think you are. God will come when you least expect it, and in a guise you hardly recognize, and God will call your name. And if you let him come to you, you will be remade. Are you willing? The journey begins by letting go.*

Reflection Questions:

- What is your take on this encounter at a well?

- Who might you be turning from, who needs to be embraced?

- How are women empowered, or not, in your religious tradition?

Journal

6

Fierce Grace

"This being human is a guest house.
Every morning a new arrival...Welcome and entertain them all!
Even if they're a crowd of sorrows, who violently sweep
your house empty of its furniture..."

~ Rumi

By most counts I have had a good life. I've been graced with two precious children, good health, strong faith, great friends, work I love, a brother and sister who are as close to me as I am to myself. I have never known war or poverty or physical abuse. For all of this I am deeply grateful.

What I want to write about here is a time when I fell out of this life and into a place of darkness and pain – and how I learned to be grateful for that as well.

It all began on an August afternoon fifteen years ago, a Sunday afternoon to be precise. I had just come back from church, poured myself a fresh cup of coffee, gathered up the Sunday *New York Times*, and was headed toward the couch, preparing to settle down for a quiet afternoon...when all of a sudden, out of nowhere, my upper body began to burn, all through my chest and down my arms, up the back of my neck and into my scalp. I began to shake. Liquid terror poured like lava through my veins.

Somehow I made my way to the couch and sat down. I got the message that I needed to breathe, breathe deeply. And so I did – in and out, in and out. After a few minutes the symptoms subsided, and my mind began to fill with questions: What had just happened? Where had it come from? What should I do?

I had separated two months earlier from my husband of twenty-three years. And while I was greatly saddened by the loss, I had been coping surprisingly well on my own. Until now.

Our marriage had been challenging from the start; and as time wore on our wants and needs grew increasingly incompatible. Love frayed; resentments multiplied; emotional cruelties occurred; real damage was done. Over the years the situation became a source of anguish to me. Perhaps to him as well.

My hope, in separating, had been to give us both time and space to get clear about what was happening to us, and what was being asked of us as two people who could no longer honor our vows without swallowing our selves. No lawyer had been hired, no contracts drawn up, but it was clear our life together could not go on as before.

Over time with reluctance, and with real trepidation, I

let myself realize that the marriage was over. To go on would have been to betray my self and risk losing my life. I believe it was Eugene O'Neil who warned against dying with our music still in us. I knew if I stayed that would happen to me. And so I left.

I quickly became caught up with building my new life – finding and furnishing a small apartment, giving new creative energy to my work, making time to be with my children as they worked through their feelings, finding in my friends and family wellsprings of love and support, experiencing a profound new level of trust in the God of my life. Not the God of my childhood whose teachings on the subject of divorce were unequivocal, but the God I had come to know through years of prayer and study and spiritual direction, a God who called me to choose life, whatever the cost. "I have come that you may have life," Jesus says, "and have it abundantly."

Yes, curious as it may sound, I had felt God with me from the very beginning of this long and painful process, giving me eyes to see, strength to speak, courage to act. For too many years I had lived caught between the need to comply and the call to be true. The truth was that this marriage was in critical condition and all attempts to get help only made things worse. And yet I'd been taught that, short of abuse or abandonment, divorce was not an option. You stayed whether you liked it or not, and made the best of what you had. Never mind that you were being drained dry.

Grace came in the freedom I felt to go against my conditioning, to trust my inner knowing, to do what had to be done. It was God who helped me give up my illusions; to overcome my attachment to being "a good wife"; for once in my life to give integrity the priority it deserved. (Fortunately our financial resources were sufficient to guarantee that neither of us would suffer a dramatic change in lifestyle after the divorce – not an incidental consideration.)

And so, here I was two months later, grieving the loss but also full of gratitude and hope for the future. My husband had come to a place of acceptance and was getting on with his life. Even my children, 19 and 21 at the time, once the shock had been absorbed, began to experience a new freedom in making choices for their own lives.

So far, so good.

Then comes this day, this ordinary August afternoon, when with no warning and for no apparent reason, a tidal wave hits, blowing out windows, flooding floors, sending solid objects flying through the air like toys. I am left in pieces, shattered to the core.

It took a long time and a lot of help, but little by little I put myself back together again. Though I never will know exactly what happened or why, I was given a possible cause and a way to live through to the other side. What I learned in therapy was that the incident – so raw, so primal – was most likely related to an early traumatic experience buried deep in my unconscious. The marriage had functioned as a kind of container, a stabilizer. Ending the marriage broke the container, leaving me exposed to these dark forces – forces that needed to be brought to consciousness if I was ever to heal and become more whole.

It wasn't the surfacing of this material that was the problem. It was the fact that it happened all at once, and with no skilled therapist to regulate the process. The unconscious erupted like a volcano, overwhelming my capacity to cope.

As puzzling as this verdict was to me, something about it felt right. Also I preferred it to the alternative – that I was simply going nuts.

It took nearly a year to regain my footing. And I could not have done it without help from doctors, therapists, family, and friends. Their love and care saved my life. When I couldn't be alone, there would always be a room in someone's home for the night. I remember one especially unbearable night, lying awake in the guest bedroom of my friend Trisha's house, drenched in sweat, my heart pounding, my mind in turmoil. I'd been through many nights like this, but for some reason this particular night I didn't see how I could get through to morning. So I did what I absolutely did not want to do. I got up, went downstairs, woke up my friend and asked if she could sit with me for a little while.

Right away, she rose from her bed, pulled a shawl from the back of her chair and put it around my shoulders. She took two rosaries from her dresser drawer and walked with me to the living room where she set me down in a chair, lit a candle, and went to the kitchen to make a pot of Chamomile tea. In a few minutes she returned with the tea and together we prayed the rosary. "Hail Mary full of grace, the Lord is with Thee..." Just before dawn I returned to my room and fell asleep.

Another of God's tender mercies to me in that time came in the form of a Maryknoll sister, living in a contemplative community in upstate New York. She was widely known as an intuitive healer and a gifted spiritual director. A dear friend who had worked with her for years gave powerful testimony to her healing power and suggested I give her a call.

At first I resisted. After all, what could she do? She didn't even know me. But as my weight dropped, my hair thinned, and the sleepless nights reached critical proportions, I realized the danger I was in and decided to give it a try. My hope was now in God alone, and it felt as if this might be of God.

I placed the call one morning from my office. She answered on the first ring. I introduced myself and mentioned my friend who had given me her name. "How can I help you?" she asked, so gently. I began to speak, and as my story poured out, a vast inexplicable relief came over me. I told her about the separation and impending divorce, about the breakdown and my fear that there was something terribly wrong with me. When I had finished, she thanked me for trusting her with my story, then said: "The first thing you need to know is that there is nothing wrong with you. Nothing at all. This is simply a part of your journey, a critical part, a difficult time, but rich with possibilities. Things are happening just as they should." Yes, the pain was very bad — she used the term "raw" — but I could trust that what felt like death was in reality the path to life.

She encouraged me to continue doing whatever was helpful: working with my therapist, taking medication, avoiding stress as much as possible. "Don't judge or interpret your experience," she cautioned. "Simply live it. Try to see it as part of your process, and trust that it will come to an end, leaving you more whole on the other side." She said I would be well again "sooner than you think."

She never suggested this was part of God's plan, that somehow God had caused this crisis to precipitate the breakdown that would lead to a breakthrough. Absolutely not. Rather she invited me to stop trying to figure out why it happened or what to do about it. I was simply to trust in God's love and God's power to attend me as I made my way in the dark, recovering a vital piece of myself in the process. She spoke about how deeply present God was to me in my suffering, not as bystander but as compassionate companion, sharing the pain, supporting me with countless graces.

And in time all she prophesied came true.

I have a life now that belongs to me. It's not perfect but it gives me great joy. I admit there are times when I feel overwhelmed and am tempted to trade my "wild and precious" life for a safe harbor. But those times don't last long. And even if I wanted to go back, there's way too much of me now to bend myself back in place.

Years ago I read a lovely memoir by Swedish actress Liv Ullman. The book was called *Changes*. In it Ms. Ullman talks about her decision to reclaim her life, to stop relying on others to keep her safe, to make her happy. Below is an excerpt from that book. It came to my attention recently when I was flipping through one of my old journals dating back to 1975. I share it here, as I close this reflection, because it says so simply what I mean.

From Ms. Ullman: "I found respect when I became independent, ceased to cling. Ceased to rely so desperately on others for my happiness...I found pleasure in my newfound ability to make my own decisions (even when they were bad), took delight in my work, in being angry, in weeping, in laughing, in living...I was often afraid...But I was richer within; I was better friends with myself...I used to want to lodge in someone's pocket and be able to jump in and out whenever it suited me. Now I go around listening for cries from other women who I imagine are locked in other's pockets."

I spent the first half of my life in someone else's pocket.

It took courage to step out, to leave behind what was uncomfortable but familiar. It took trusting in the God of my life to see me through. It took learning how to live with the exposure, then coming to love the open air. This journey from bondage to freedom is not without cost, we all know that. It is in fact the "pearl of great price." But what is more important than getting one's life back? Than knowing you won't have to die with your music still in you?

Reflection Questions:

- Have you ever experienced a fierce grace in your life?

- What was your sense of God's presence/absence in the process?

- What have you learned that could help you in companioning others in dark times?

Journal

_____
_____
_____
_____
_____
_____
_____
_____
_____
_____
_____
_____
_____
_____
_____
_____
_____
_____
_____
_____
_____
_____
_____

Journal

7

MY SISTER MY SELF

"When you listen generously to people, they can hear the truth in themselves, often for the first time."

~ Rachel Naomi Remen

I have always loved spending time with my sister. She's funny, smart, curious, kind, and she has been blessed with a very special skill: she knows how to listen. She listens the way an artist paints, with full attention.

She is especially precious to me in times of trouble. No matter what the issue is – a misunderstanding with one of the children, a troubling situation at work, a worry over some symptom in my aging body – I know I can go to her, and after we talk I will feel better. Much better.

Not because anything has changed. Except that now I feel lighter, calmer, braver, more able to be with what is going on. You might say, I go in like a caterpillar and come out like a butterfly.

How does it work? It's the way she listens, pure and simple. With her I know I can take all the time I need. She won't get impatient, restless, or distracted. She won't interrupt, ask questions, give me her opinion, try to fix things. She may give advice, but only when I ask. She trusts that I have what it takes to work things out, in a way that's right for me.

When I pause, she doesn't jump in to fill the silence. She waits...and in that accepting silence I'm reassured that this is a space where I am safe. She really is here for me.

The quality of her listening encourages me to descend deeper into what is going on, to get it all out, and when I'm ready, to begin exploring my alternatives. In her presence I find myself saying things I didn't know I knew. Spiritual writers have a name for this gift of time and space. They call it a "ministry of presence," and the experience is full of grace.

What touches me most is her ability to set aside her own agenda, to empty herself of judgments and just be deeply present to me and my experience. She "takes off her shoes," you might say, to enter into my reality. It is the ultimate kindness.

Unfortunately this experience of being heard is rare. It seems we don't have time these days. We care, of course, but we are just too busy to sit still and make ourselves available to one another. Besides, if you're like me, you've gotten awfully fond of the sound of your own voice.

Steven Covey, in his book *Seven Habits of Highly Effective People*, says that what usually happens when one person speaks is that others don't really listen. They pretend to listen, but are thinking mostly about how to respond. While the other speaks, they busy themselves evaluating (deciding if they agree or disagree). When they do speak they give unsolicited advice based on their experience, which is about as useful as giving a person your eyeglasses to help them see.

Good listeners are rare. Listening is hard work. It takes discipline and self-restraint. In my practice as a spiritual director I am trained to listen. All day long this is my work, my joy. Yet even so, there are times I find myself battling the urge to take over, to tell my directees what they need to do. Fortunately I am blessed to have my sister close at hand. She keeps me mindful of the ways deep listening creates a climate where I can be empowered to heal myself, to find my own way.

My job now is to pass it on, to work at becoming a better listener myself, not just in my work but in my after-hours life as well. I think of how I am in my own family, with the people I love best in all the world – how busy I am getting things done for them, as if we lived by bread alone. Perhaps I need to give more time to simply being there, present to them, as if I had all the time in the world, making space where they too may enter in as caterpillars and come out like butterflies.

Reflection Questions:

- When was the last time you felt truly listened to?

- What happens when you experience this blessing?

- Who in your life needs a good listening to?

Journal

_____

_____

_____

_____

_____

_____

_____

_____

_____

_____

_____

_____

_____

_____

_____

_____

_____

_____

_____

_____

_____

_____

_____

8

JAPANESE MAPLE

*"The world is charged with the grandeur of God.
It will flame out, like shining from shook foil."*

~ Gerard Manley Hopkins

I could tell from her expression as she studied the chest X-ray that the news was not good. "How long have you been sick?" she asked, still intent on the screen.

"Well, I've been feeling a bit dragged out lately, but it wasn't until the weekend that I started feeling really sick, and when I took my temperature and saw it was 102, I decided I'd better come see you."

She turned to face me. "I'm glad you did. You've got double pneumonia."

"But I don't feel that sick," I replied.

"Well you are," she said firmly. "I'm going to start you on an antibiotic, and I'll need to check you again in three days." The implication was that if things weren't better by then I would have to be hospitalized.

"Have you been under a lot of stress lately?" she asked.

"I have been pretty busy," I replied. In truth I was exhausted. I'd been going non- stop for weeks.

"Well, whatever you've got on the calendar, cancel it," she said as she wrote out my prescription. "Your only assignment now is to take your medicine and rest. Drink lots of liquids. Don't go out. And I'll see you back here on Thursday."

On my way home I stopped at the pharmacy to pick up my "Z-Pac," When I got home, I poured myself a glass of juice and made my way upstairs to the bedroom. I peeled off my clothes and dropped my softest nightie down over my head. The room was bright with sunlight. I went to close the blinds, then decided to leave them open, to let in the warmth and light.

After setting my half-empty glass on the nightstand, I climbed into bed, drew the covers up around my shoulders, closed my eyes and let myself drift off to sleep. For the next two days that pattern pretty much prevailed – drinking and sleeping and waking, and working my way through my powerful pills.

On the third day I returned to the doctor. She checked my lungs and said I needed to stay home a few more days. Apparently the bug was weaker but wasn't done with me yet.

I came home, made up my bed and moved to an armchair by the window, looking out over the backyard. And that is when the beauty began.

As word got out that I was confined to my room, kindness

came from all directions. Friends stopped by with homemade soup, fresh flowers, bread and cheese, and gourmet chocolate bars. Clients whose appointments I had had to cancel wrote with promises of prayer. My sons made themselves available for shopping and sitting.

In this circle of care I had only one thing to do: to rest. Eat a little, pray a little, read a little, rest. As the days went by, I found myself, not bored and restless as I had expected, but more and more entranced by all the living things in my backyard – trees, bushes, lacy ferns, chatty squirrels, birds. Now that I wasn't in a hurry to go anywhere, I could be where I was – simply be. All morning I looked. I looked and looked. And as the hours went by, my looking turned to gazing. It all began to feel like prayer.

Gazing had become a portal, opening me to the shimmer in things. I was especially taken by a Japanese maple tree that had lived happily for twelve years in my backyard. I planted it when I first moved into the house, in memory of my mother. The tree had flourished, growing huge over the years, becoming quite a diva, Grand Dame of the Garden.

At first I saw her as just a lovely tree, but as I got to know her over hours and days of gazing, in shade and sun, light streaming through her lacey fingers, her fragile branches bobbing in the breeze, dripping wet in the morning rain, drying herself in the afternoon sun, she came to life. It was almost as if my mother had come back to be with me in this exquisite tree.

My sensible self would never put up with this interpretation, of course. To her this is just a tree. But all those days of living quietly and learning how to look and see, argued for me. Yes, it's a tree, but a tree with a great gift for those with eyes to see. It brought my mother back, to tend to me.

Poet/mystic Gerard Manley Hopkins tells us the world is full of the grandeur of God; it flashes out "like shining from shook foil." Where is this shining of which he speaks? Why not here? Why not now? Maybe the shining goes on all the time, and now and then we're given eyes to see it. Maybe it's only when life grinds to a halt that we give ourselves the time to look and see. To see and receive.

I am back to work now; my gazing days are over. But once in a while a beam of light will fall across my path and stop me, or the song of a bird will thrill me as I trot down the driveway in my bathrobe to retrieve the morning paper. Yes, now and then I feel the warmth, catch a flash of the light, know the Love that is real and alive and right here, right now.

As I finish this piece, my cat Martin jumps into my lap, insisting he be recognized as one more way God loves. Why yes, of course. Yes indeed.

Reflection Questions:

• What is your relationship to the word "rest"?

• How do you rest?
  If you don't rest, what keeps you from doing so?

• How does the "shining" show up in your life?

Journal

_____

_____

_____

_____

_____

_____

_____

_____

_____

_____

_____

_____

_____

_____

_____

_____

_____

_____

_____

_____

_____

_____

_____

_____

_____

Journal

9

BEGINNERS BEWARE

*"My mother lived a life of terrible hardship
and she never fought back. She was completely unable
to distinguish between kinds of hardship, between
what was unavoidable and what might be avoided...
Things were the way they were – and that was God's will."*

~ Sanford/Donovan, *Women and Self-Esteem*

I am dealing here with a slippery subject. After countless attempts to nail things down, I have decided to simply plunge in, hoping you will stay with me as I twist and turn, trying to find firm ground on which to stand. I want to explore with you some thoughts on the place of suffering in the lives of faithful Christians.

In my own life, in the lives of those who raised me, in the lives of some of the people I serve now in spiritual direction, I have noticed a troubling inclination to see suffering as good for us. That may be too strong. But there is at least some confusion about God's will for us here on earth. Are we supposed to be happy? Are we allowed to enjoy our life? Or does God want us to deny ourselves, endure whatever is given without complaint – as a way to prove our love and purify ourselves for eternity?

What started this odd ball rolling was a conversation I had with a friend recently about my work habits. I was saying how, when I did my writing, I liked to go to the local coffee shop and watch the world go by while I worked, even though I was pretty sure I'd work better if I stayed home alone.

She looked at me with a wry smile, then shook her head and said: "Why do you always think harder is better?" I put my cup down with a thud. She started laughing. "Remember the time you told me you thought your morning prayer would be more worthwhile if you hauled yourself out of bed at 6:00 a.m. to say it? What's that about? Where does it come from?"

I thought back to my Irish Catholic upbringing (for which I am deeply grateful but which did have a killjoy tinge to it – thanks to the influence of Jansenism). Sure enough in those days, and for good reason, life was expected to be hard, pleasures few and far between. A popular prayer of my childhood "Hail Holy Queen," spoke of the faithful as "poor banished children of Eve, mourning and weeping in this vale of tears."

Not only was suffering seen as inevitable; if patiently endured it could be seen as a pathway to heaven. Just as Jesus had shown his love for us by dying on a cross, so we could show our love for God by meekly accepting whatever was given us to bear. In the Gospel of Matthew 16:24 Jesus actually says: "If any want to become my followers, let them deny themselves and take up their cross and follow me." It's hard not to assume from this that sacrifice and self-denial were the hallmarks of a good Christian.

To be sure, as Christians we are called to live generous lives, to struggle with that willful part of us that wants things our own way. But our struggle is in the service of a good life, full of peace and joy and generosity. The God who made us knows that unbridled willfulness leads in the end to misery.

Ours is not a God who requires suffering but a God whose heart breaks when we suffer. Ours is a God whose life on earth in Jesus was all about alleviating suffering wherever he found it.

Perhaps the reason it means so much to me to have this conversation – to sort out the difference between suffering that leads to life and suffering that stifles and deforms – is because I saw how an unnuanced interpretation of this call to bear the cross had led people I loved to lead less-than lives, out of a mistaken notion that God would be pleased by their sacrifice.

When tragedies struck in my house growing up, they were seen as a part of God's plan. When, for example, my mother's mother lost two children in childbirth, she accepted the loss as God's will, which gave her some peace but also left her wondering what she'd done to deserve such a harsh punishment. When my grandmother's own mother was dying of cancer, her way of making meaning of the pain was to believe it was meant to prepare her for the Afterlife. When asked how she could bear it, her reply was, "I'd rather suffer on this side than on the other."

In their defense, life was harsh in those days. Suffering was plentiful, and seeing it as divinely ordained must have made it more bearable. I admire the dignity and courage of my parents and their forebears, their willingness to accept what they didn't want and work with what they had. I admire their confidence that God was with them and that He knew best.

But I can't help feeling gravely uncomfortable with the suggestion that God causes babies to be stillborn, or inflicts pain on elderly people to punish or prepare them for the life to come.

I remember being thrilled the day my mother, who never spent money on herself, broke down and bought a gold velveteen couch she had been eyeing for months in the window of our neighborhood furniture store. That couch gave her such pleasure over the years. And it was meant for her; we all knew that. But she never got over feeling faintly guilty for having been so "extravagant."

She was a great spirit, my mother, with a hearty appetite for life. She loved fun and fancy things, but it made her uncomfortable to have "too much." Wealth was seen as suspect; doing things just for pleasure made her feel uncomfortable. After she died and we were cleaning out her apartment, I found in the back of her sweater drawer an unopened bottle of Joy perfume wrapped in an old washcloth.

I remember when a beloved uncle was diagnosed in his 50's with an acute anxiety disorder that had made his life a living hell – he was encouraged to seek psychiatric help, but could never bring himself to make the call. I suppose his reluctance had partly to do with feeling ashamed. But I can't help wondering if on some level he was reluctant to seek healing because he felt it was too much to ask. Suppose he had been given this cross to bear? Then he was meant to bear it. Like Jesus bore his.

He was a deeply spiritual man, my uncle. One of his treasured possessions was a copy of Thomas à Kempis' *Imitation of Christ*. It was given to me when he died. From the little I read, it seemed the author was suggesting that by embracing our suffering, we unite ourselves with Christ. Now I'm sure Thomas à Kempis meant no harm; and I do realize that many of the greatest saints did willingly embrace lives of great suffering out of love for God and the world. But to a person like my uncle, inclined to ask nothing for himself, this theology only supported a profoundly disabling approach to life. As Father Thomas Keating puts it in one of his CDs on Centering Prayer: "Renunciation is the last thing people with low self-esteem need to hear!"

Perhaps books like Thomas à Kempis' don't have to go, but

they might need to come with a warning label: **Beginners Beware**. Radical self-emptying is not a recommended way of life for everyday people. While it may be a legitimate call for a select few, it presumes that the one being called makes the choice freely, from a whole self firmly grounded in the Living God, and does so for love alone. To make this a general instruction for all God's faithful leaves people who love life in a terrible bind.

I know for myself as a child growing up, I got snagged many times on these mixed messages. I wanted to be good, to do God's will; but I wanted a lovely life as well. Somehow the two seemed incompatible. Which would it be? Was it wrong to want nice things and have good times? Not that I'd refuse to bear my share of suffering, but did I have to go looking for it?

Fortunately, thanks to my grandfather, whose God loved life and loved me too, I was able to hold onto a vision of God as good to us, and Jesus as one who came that we might have life. But that didn't keep me from leaving the Church when I was twenty one.

I was gone for fifteen years. During that time I fell for the equally unreal message being pedaled by the secular culture – that suffering was unnecessary and avoidable. Getting our needs met was the name of the game. The irony, of course, is that this way of life doesn't work either. Refusing to suffer is just the flip side of seeking it out. Either way we lose.

Eventually God graced me with a host of holy people who helped me find my way back to a place within the tradition where I could stand.

In sum: Clearly suffering should not be sought, should not be sanctified for its own sake. On the other hand, suffering that must be borne can be transformative. Times of unavoidable pain in my life, when I am able to live them deeply, have opened me to Love like nothing else can.

Perhaps it is simply a question of discernment. Some things have to be gotten through the best way we know how. My friend who's undergoing chemotherapy for breast cancer – she has no choice. But what about another friend who refuses to leave an abusive marriage because she believes God has called her to stay and pray? Here the God-filled choice is far less clear.

The challenge is to believe that our God wants fullness of life for us all, and any situation that cripples us is not God's will. When we are in doubt about what to do, we pray for guidance: is this a situation I am called to endure or to change? Then we ask for the strength and support to do what feels true.

Above all, we trust God's presence with us in the process, this wondrous God who wants only to lead us to life, not later but right here and now.

Reflection Questions:

- What was your own religious upbringing like –
positives and negatives?

- How do you interpret Jesus' command to take
up your cross?

- What do you think of this statement by
Teilhard de Chardin:
*"Joy is the most infallible sign of the presence of
God"*?

Journal

_____

_____

_____

_____

_____

_____

_____

_____

_____

_____

_____

_____

_____

_____

_____

_____

_____

_____

_____

_____

_____

_____

_____

_____

_____

_____

_____

_____

_____

10

BECOMING ALL PRAYER

"What you do matters – but not much.
What you are matters tremendously."

~ Catherine de Hueck Doherty

When a person comes for spiritual direction, one of the first questions we are taught to ask is: "Tell me about your prayer life." A fair question, wouldn't you think? If someone is seeking spiritual direction, it stands to reason we would want to know something about how they pray. And they would want to tell us.

It is meant to be a gentle question, one that will help open the conversation. There is no correct answer. As spiritual directors we are just as comfortable with, "I have no formal prayer life," as we are with, "I pray regularly, three times a day." For us their response is simply a point of entry.

What interests me – and why I have stopped using this as an opening question – is that often people hear it not as a genuine question but as a veiled attempt to determine how devout they are. Or aren't. They experience it as a test, one they are about to flunk.

Even those with well-established practices feel they aren't doing enough. Surely they could do more, do better. Barbara Brown Taylor, one of our generation's most wise and holy women, admitted during a talk on her book *An Altar in the World*, that she would "rather talk about my fondness for Bombay Sapphire gin martinis than my prayer life." It brought the house down!

Where does this come from, this uneasiness around the condition of our prayer life? I am no different than anyone else. I too am never satisfied. When I go over the hour set for prayer, I tell myself I took too much time. When I get up late and have to be quick, I didn't take enough. Or I didn't go deep. Or I missed three times this week. On and on it goes. Meanwhile, the gracious God of my life sits patiently by, hoping for my company.

One way to begin making our way out of this thicket is to remember what we know: that this dear God who loves us so has no requirements. Really! She doesn't give tests. We can never get an "A"; nor would she dream of flunking us, no matter how pathetic our attempts to pray might be. Our performance is the last thing on Her mind.

What She wants most of all is to be with us – with us and for us – and to make of us a place where Her Spirit can dwell. "Abide in me," Jesus says, "as I abide in you." A prayerful person is one who has said Yes to this tender invitation, and goes about making ready the soil of her soul. What this looks like will vary from person to person, from time to time. One day she may be able to sit in quiet prayer for an hour or more; another, she may be lucky to run off an Our Father in the shower. That's just how it goes. God knows.

I met with a woman once who came to me convinced that God was fed up with her. She had high standards for her prayer life, as she did for everything else, and felt she never managed to meet them. Her opening instruction to me as her new spiritual director was to "hold my feet to the fire." Each session was to be a kind of confession. She would come in and talk about her progress (or her failure to progress), and my job was to praise her or forgive her, and encourage her to try harder.

Over time, as we came to know and trust each other, she let me open some windows on her way of understanding prayer. Yes, saying the rosary and reading the Bible were certainly valid, time-honored ways to pray. Sitting in silence for twenty minutes twice a day is a good and holy thing, no doubt about it. But not all lives allow for that. Also, if we are called to "pray ceaselessly," then mustn't prayer be more than saying words? Prayer must be a way of life, and life must offer ways to pray all day.

When she spoke one day about how she felt close to God in her garden, I asked if she could consider the love and care with which she tended her plants as a form of prayer. She looked interested. I continued. "What about the other day – when you decided to put down the newspaper you'd looked forward to reading all day, to listen to your granddaughter tell you in great detail about her day?" She smiled. I told her about my weekend, walking in the woods. How I sat for an hour under a tree in the silence of the forest, breathing in the fragrance of fertile things and feeling so grateful for all of it. Was that not prayer?

How about when we think to whisper "thank you," as we fill the trunk of our car with bags of fresh groceries? What about when your heartache over a child who is suffering or a friend who is dying wakes you in the night and you go down to the den and stand before the sliding glass doors and stare at the moon and weep? Isn't this also prayer?

Isn't prayer possible anytime, anywhere? Isn't prayer less about what we do than who we are? Isn't it fair to say that whatever we do, if we do it with love and attention, can be a form of prayer? The Buddhists think so. They call it mindfulness. St Benedict thought so. His famous Rule of Life insists that prayer need never stop. Attending with care to the work of the day is as sacred as praying Compline in the chapel.

I have on my desk a postcard with the picture of an egret standing motionless at the edge of a pond. The quote underneath is by Benedictine Sister Joan Chittister: "Awareness of the present moment puts us in the presence of God wherever we are." Mary Oliver in her poem, "The Summer Day," says it this way: "I don't know exactly what a prayer is. I do know how to pay attention..."

So where does all this leave us?

Ideally, to become a person of prayer, it seems to me we need both structured prayer times and a practice of attending to God's presence throughout the day. Structured prayer is the "lattice" that supports our day. Praying the psalms, pondering the day's Scripture readings, sitting quietly in God's presence – these intentional practices help secure God's place at the center of our busy days, strengthening our ability to attend, to choose well, whatever the day brings.

Once we leave our chair and enter the day, our prayer takes the shape of presence. We become salt for the earth, bread for the world. In the end it is all about kindness.

I remember Sister Mary telling me once that prayer is meant above all to transform us. "I don't care if a person spends hours on their knees every day and sees visions," she said. "If they're not kind, I'm not impressed."

Reflection Questions:

- What is your definition of prayer?

- When do you feel most prayerful?

- How does it feel to think of becoming a prayer?

Journal

11

A Jewel in the Cave

"If I say, 'Surely the darkness shall cover me, and the light around me become night,' even the darkness is not dark to you, and night is as bright as the day..."

~ Psalm 139

In my work as a spiritual director I am often called to walk with people into the deep end of their lives, to companion them as they wrestle with questions of faith and meaning. I work with men and women, young and old, counselors, ministers, executives, homemakers, students, retirees. What they all have in common is a thirst for God and a desire to live in tune with Love's call.

Sometimes our work is simply being curious – looking to discern God's gracious movements in the ordinary events of their everyday lives. Sometimes we walk in joy and gratitude for answered prayers, gratuitous gifts, awakenings. Now and then, when life hits hard below the belt and they come in staggering from the blow, our work is to stay together in the dark, praying and waiting for glimpses of light.

This work is never easy. Life can tear us up and pitch us into godforsaken places, with only agony, rage, terror, emptiness, to keep us company. A daughter is raped; a dear friend is fatally injured in a car crash; an addict we have known and loved gives up the fight; a marriage of many years falls apart without warning; the doctor calls to say the test results are in and the cancer has come back.

What now?

Dutch Jesuit Henri Nouwen, who struggled for years with severe depression, says we must find some way to dwell in the darkness – stay with it, pray with it, raise our fists, cry out our pain. And wait in faith. Wait for the blessing that will surely come, "the jewel in the cave."

Three stories come to mind.

Years ago my son lost a classmate to cancer at nineteen. He was with the boy in the hospital just before he died. The boy's mother and several of his friends were there as well. "I was holding his hand," he told me later. "He seemed agitated, frightened. He kept asking, 'Why am I here?' He had no peace, no special understanding. He was as shocked as we were by what was happening to him."

My son turned to look at me, holding inside the unspoken question.

I told him I didn't understand why these things happened, but I knew it wasn't because God wanted it that way, or because He didn't care and simply turned away. I said our faith teaches us that God was present in that room, right in the midst of the pain. Not to cure him but to sustain him. And if we could somehow believe that, it would make the things we have to bear more bearable. I told him how his willingness to be with his friend, to sit beside him, to reach out and take his hand and listen while he spoke his fear and anguish out loud – that was one way God was present to his friend. "Through you," I said.

I remember in my own life years ago, being with a friend when she got a phone call from her sister in Ireland telling her that her beloved younger brother had just been shot to death in a gun battle in Belfast. I remember her face when she hung up the phone. I remember reaching out to her, through air as thick as glue. I remember how she came to me, and how we sank together onto the couch and how I held her hard and rocked her back and forth. And all I could say, over and over, was, "I'm sorry...I'm so sorry."

Later, when I was able to get her the money for her plane ticket and take her to the airport, I felt like I had finally done something. Little did I know that the money was something but the holding was everything.

I once worked with a woman in spiritual direction who at sixty was diagnosed with terminal cancer. She was told she had only months to live. She was a woman of deep faith, who understood that life's terms weren't always fair, and she had accepted her fate. What was causing her great anguish was not the thought of dying, not even the fear of suffering, but the apparent absence of God in the midst of her pain. (Never mind that this experience of abandonment is common among God's chosen ones, including Jesus himself in his final hour on the cross. In Mother Teresa's private journals, published after her death, readers were shocked to find that she too went for years with no felt sense of God's love.)

My client recounted one hellish night in the emergency room. "As I lay on the stretcher, waiting to be taken to a room, listening to the doctors talk about me as if I weren't there, I felt cold and sick and so afraid. I called on God to be with me. I asked for the grace to feel His presence. That was all I asked. I asked it over and over and over. And nothing changed. No one came. All night I lay there pleading for His company. It was just so awful. "Where are you?" I prayed. "Come to me."

She paused, then looked up at me, her eyes brimming with tears, asking without words if I could withstand her despair. I waited, open to whatever she needed to say. "Maybe there is no God," she whispered. "Maybe it's just a story we tell ourselves to feel less alone."

I want to say, "O no, it's not made up. God is real. God is present, more so than ever in times of suffering." But in all these years of doing the work, I have learned not to push people. She will find her way, in her own time. Besides, God doesn't need to be defended. I know without a doubt that I can trust God in this experience of desolation as surely as I trust Him in times of consolation.

"Can you say more about your experience?" I ask. "Can you tell God how you felt." She hesitates, then speaks softly: "I want to know...Where were you?" she says in a whisper. Then louder, "Where were you?" And finally, "WHERE WERE YOU?" The dam breaks and the pain pours out.

After a while it's over and we sit together in the silence. I reach for her hand and cover it with mine. The air feels soft and faintly fragrant. For now there is nothing more to say.

She calls me from home a few days later to tell me she has taken my suggestion to keep talking with God in her journal. "I tell him everything, how angry and afraid I was, how this experience has shaken my faith. At first it felt wrong. How could I talk to God like that? But after awhile I felt better. It was as if God were with me...close by...wanting me to say it... leaning in and listening."

In time she did heal, and space was cleared for a deeper intimacy with God than she had ever known. Not the God of her childhood who reigns on high but the God who is Emmanuel, God with us, sharing her joys, bearing her pain, bringing her from death back to life.

That was my experience as well, as I struggled through a breakdown after my divorce. (See "Fierce Grace.") I was able to hold out hope for her because I had survived a desperate time myself. I knew what it was like to feel utterly alone, to thrash around, call for help, beg God to find me, and get no response.

Relief came when I learned to let go of needing things to be different, and simply let myself be with the fear and the pain. As I became accustomed to the experience, I saw that I could stand it; it wouldn't overwhelm me. The sleeplessness, the panic attacks, the fear of being left alone – none of that went away. But by accepting these symptoms as part of my reality, and letting myself go to God to speak freely about the experience, I was freed from the hysteria which only ground me deeper into the muck. Oddly enough, accepting things as they were calmed me. As I grew more still, I began to recognize the angels hovering in the shadows, ambassadors of God who had been there all along.

Toward the end of my "time of trial," I even came to embrace the experience as a critical part of my journey. By living it as it was given me to live, I became stronger and acquired priceless life learnings.

Suffering is never easy. Being with people we care about who suffer can be even worse. We want so much to help, to make it go away. But in my years of being with suffering people who've chosen to live their lives in God, I see that our work is not to try to get them out of it – we can't – but to be willing to enter in, to meet them in their "tomb of pain" (Ann Weems' *Psalms of Lament*) and hold the lamp of hope, while we search for the Light that burns at the heart of all things.

When they are able hear it, we tell them they will make it through; one way or another life will meet them on the other side. Perhaps not soon. And not without pain. But it is true. One day they will be born again. I see it happen all the time.

Reflection Questions:

- Think of a dark time in your life.
  Was there a jewel in your cave?

- What sustained you while you waited?

- How have dark times challenged/changed
  your image of God?

Journal

Journal

Arko Datta

12

KYTHING:
A WAY TO HOLD THEM

"The righteous perish and no one takes it to heart."
~ Isaiah 57

Some days it's hard to read the newspaper. So much poverty, violence, sickness, unspeakable suffering. So many people all over the world who've been driven out of their homes and have nowhere to go. Forced to leave with only the clothes on their backs and the few household goods they can wrap in a blanket. Children in their arms, clutching their skirts, walking for days without water or food. It is almost unbearable to think what they are going through; I can't imagine what it is like to live it.

Back several years ago, when the tsunami hit Thailand, I remember being captivated by a picture of a Thai woman, a victim of the catastrophe. She was lying face down on the ground, her arms outstretched, her hands turned toward the sky. She is beyond terror, beyond grief, lost in a desolation deeper than any words can express. Her whole life had just been torn away.

She comes to mind now, as images of endless streams of refugees from war torn countries fill our screens and newspapers. She comes now not so much as one particular woman, though she is surely that, but as an icon of Christ crucified again and again in the suffering of Her people.

When I first saw the picture, I must confess I looked and looked again, then turned away. But I couldn't forget her. Later in the day I found myself retrieving the image, printing out a copy, and placing it on my prayer table, between a blue porcelain angel my older son had given me for Christmas and a pewter plate that reads: "The light of God surrounds you. The love of God enfolds you."

Somehow I needed to be with her. I wanted her to know... To know what? That I noticed? That I care? That what happened to her mattered to me? What difference would that make?

I remember sitting down to pray on that first night and having the word "kything" come to mind. It was a term I hadn't thought of in years, not since reading Madeleine L'Engle's classic story, *A Wind in the Door*, to my children. Kything is the term L'Engle uses to describe the wordless way the cherubim – and a few enlightened humans – communicate. It is a deep intuitive communing, heart to heart, soul to soul. When Meg "kythes" with her absent brother Charles Wallace, she seems to be with him, "not in person, but in her heart."

I realize that I am being invited to kythe with this woman. But I have no idea what that means. In conversation with a friend over lunch the next day she tells me about a book she has had in her bookshelf for years and never read. It's on the subject of kything. (Imagine that!) She is quick to offer it to me.

The book, published in 1988, is by Lawrence Savary and Patricia Berne: *Kything: The Art of Spiritual Presence*. The purpose of kything, they say, is to channel God's healing energy to people in need – across time and space, to people we know and people we don't know, to people alive and those who have crossed over. It doesn't require any elaborate training or special skill, just a loving heart and a desire to connect with the world's suffering people on God's behalf. Children can kythe as well as adults. They may be even better at it, since they don't have to know how it works.

If I agree to assume the task of praying for this woman in this way, I am invited to follow a simple, step-by-step process: I begin by getting relaxed and centered. I become aware of God's loving presence and bring to mind the anguished woman. I affirm my desire to connect with her in her suffering, and offer a simple prayer for her and her people. Then I visualize God's love surrounding, consoling and strengthening her. Somehow my willingness to be present to her in this way opens us both to God's power.

Over time, I'm sad to say, the practice faded away. Why?

Not for lack of subjects; not because I lost faith in the practice. To be perfectly honest, I got bored with it – doing the same thing day in and day out with no seeable results. I don't know what happened to that woman. But I do know, as I write this, that I am being called to start again, and this time to stick with it. Without knowing what a difference it makes, without needing to know.

And so, as they say, the choice is mine: to look away or stay and pray.

Lately I've taken to collecting pictures of suffering people. I listen as they speak of what it's like for them, as we sit together, me in my cozy house in my quiet neighborhood, with food in the larder and money in the bank; them, God knows where. And I am assured that in this connection something good is being born – in them and in me. For the suffering ones a sense, I hope, that they are not forgotten; for me, a deepening gratitude for the gift of my own life, a deepening compassion for these people who are in the end my sisters and brothers. I can't give them back their homes and families, but I can offer them a few minutes of my time, my prayer and my love. Trusting in the mysterious power of this simple act. I can thank them for the difference they have made in my life, by giving me a way to share in God's pain, to add a drop to God's ocean of care for the world.

Reflection Questions:

- What do you think of this notion of kything as a way to connect with suffering people?

- Of all the suffering people, is there one group that has a special claim on your heart?

- Are there other ways you feel called to connect with the plight of suffering people?

Journal

_____

_____

_____

_____

_____

_____

_____

_____

_____

_____

_____

_____

_____

_____

_____

_____

_____

_____

_____

_____

_____

_____

_____

Journal

13

DETERMINED DETERMINATION

"Speak your mind, even if your voice is shaking."

~ Maggie Kuhn

One of my favorite stories in all of Scripture is the story of Jesus and the Canaanite woman. I love it for so many reasons. For one thing, it's about a feisty woman who won't take no for an answer. For another, it offers us a glimpse of Jesus not as the saintly Son of God but as a fully human being, in need of being shaken loose, opened to new ways of living out his call.

Before we go into the story it's important to put it in context. Looking back several verses, we see that Jesus has been working nonstop: healing the sick, feeding the multitudes, seeking the lost, all the while trying to deal with the pesky Pharisees who keep nipping at his heels, critiquing his every move.

Just before the story begins, he is seen facing off against them. They have been fussing about dietary laws, accusing the disciples of ignoring the rules. In reply, Jesus tells them point blank that these things they are so concerned about don't matter. They idolize their traditions at the expense of their humanity. In doing so, "You break away from God."

So when we meet Jesus on the road out of town, we can safely assume he is feeling exhausted by the demands of the crowds, irritated by the pestering of the Pharisees, frustrated by the denseness of even his closest followers. He just wants to get away and rest awhile. Anyone who is familiar with the gospel knows how that goes. This day is no exception.

The story opens with Jesus "leaving that place and withdrawing to the region of Tyre and Sidon," presumably to rest and refuel before his next grueling round of healings. We see him moving down the road in the company of his disciples, when abruptly out of nowhere a distraught woman appears and starts shouting at him: "Sir, Son of David, take pity on me." She has come on behalf of her daughter who, it would seem, is in need of an exorcism. "My daughter is tormented by a devil."

What must have gone through Jesus' mind at that moment? If he was fully human as well as fully divine, one can't help but suspect that he shrank from the call. Perhaps he even picked up his pace to outrun her. He simply wasn't up to it. He had done all he could for that day. Scripture gives us simply this: "He answered her not a word."

Undeterred, she follows right behind, shouting after him.

He continues to ignore her. How long does this go on? We don't know. We do know that at some point the disciples, unnerved by her persistence, plead with Jesus to give her what she wants just so she'll go away. His response isn't at all what we would expect from this man of God. Instead of giving in to her request, he stiffens further, setting his second refusal in the context of his religious tradition: "I was sent only to the lost sheep of the House of Israel."

As if this were all it would take to turn back a mother fighting for the life of her child! Not a chance. This time, in response, she comes right up to him, kneels at his feet, and says simply: "Lord, help me." Is he looking down at her? Have their eyes met? I think not, for his next remark is utterly devoid of mercy: "It's not fair to take the food from the children's mouths and throw it to the dogs." He has just called her a dog.

Does she wince in pain, flare up in anger, give up and go home? Not at all. She steps up her game, hits the ball right back at him, and wins the point: "Even the dogs get to eat the scraps that fall from the master's table." With that, Jesus' defenses fall away. He can no longer resist opening his heart to this woman who won't go away. "Woman, great is your faith! Let it be done for you as you wish."

In this moment, the order that has been in place for centuries gets turned on its head. She becomes his teacher, he the one being taught. He will heal her daughter, and she will open his heart, revealing to him the full scope of his ministry. Her tenacity; her ferocious commitment to getting what she came for, no matter the cost; her unshakeable faith in the power of this man to heal – it rocks him. In the end, he has no choice.

Later, after the woman has left to go home to her daughter and Jesus has arrived at the place where they are going, I wonder...does he sit with the disciples around a fire, laughing about this wild wooly woman who would not go away? Does Jesus come to see the irony in this interplay? Does he remember how, earlier in the week he had chastised the Pharisees for putting tradition ahead of love's call, and here he was, about to do the same thing himself?

But unlike the Pharisees, he was willing to be converted. Instead, and this is what makes the story so remarkable and our Savior so dear and so rare, he lets this woman who doesn't qualify draw him through his resistance to a true conversion of heart. Under her influence he lets himself be moved to a radically new position. From now on, all people will be included, not just the "qualified."

My question is, how did this story ever make it into the canon – a canon put together at a time and in a culture where men were the ones in charge; women were seen and not heard. Is it possible that Jesus is once again purposely reversing the established order, giving the woman the leading role, at his expense? If I had been there in the crowd and heard the story told, it would have greatly heartened me. Did it hearten the men as well or did they wander off scratching their heads and mumbling, wondering what he'd be up to next – this odd, brave, luminous man from Galilee?

Reflection Questions:

- When in your life have you gone after what you wanted, undeterred by opposition?

- What would you say to this woman if you had the chance?

- Does the story give you new ways to think of Jesus, new ways to pray?

Journal

Journal

Marian C. Honors, CSJ

14

GOD LANGUAGE: WHY "HE" BUT NOT "SHE"?

*"As truly as God is our Father,
so just as truly is God our Mother."*
~ Julian of Norwich

When the feminist movement broke on the scene in the 1960's with the publication of Betty Friedan's *Feminine Mystique*, I was first shocked, then enthralled, and finally convicted. This was a movement long overdue. As a woman brought up in a household where women's lives were built around the needs of others, I had seen first-hand what it cost bright, ambitious women to contain themselves, to limit their living so it fit within their prescribed roles as wives and mothers, helpmates and cheerleaders.

So, when a friend invited me to join her in a study group around the subject of God language, and how our current language for God badly needed to be reformed because it supported the subordination of women, you'd think I would have jumped at the chance. Not so.

While I believed with all my heart that women had as much right as men to full lives, I couldn't see any connection between how we named God and how we treated women. I went only because my friend wouldn't take no for an answer. And I'm glad I did, though at the time, as I said, I truly could not see why it mattered. (Hard to believe how blind we can be!)

One reason I was reluctant to expose myself to this new learning was because at the time I was still attached to traditional images from my childhood, God as Lord and Master; King and Father. The image of God as Father was especially dear to me, since my own grandfather had been a gentle man from whom I had received the sweetest love growing up.

The course was held at the Aquinas Center at Emory University. The focus of our work was on the groundbreaking book, *She Who Is*, by feminist theologian Elizabeth Johnson. In it she maintains that the way we image God does matter, more than we'll ever know. It shapes the way we think about ourselves, the way we relate to one another, how we live together in community.

"The way in which a faith community shapes language about God," says Johnson, "implicitly represents what it takes to be the highest good, the profoundest truth, the most appealing beauty. Such speaking...molds the identity of the community and directs its praxis." When the predominant images for God are male, says Johnson, this works to undermine the value of the feminine and to uphold patriarchy. We need feminine imagery for God to balance the masculine imagery, says she. Otherwise, our God language supports the heretical notion that men are inherently superior to women, or at least better able to image God.

Now as I said, at the time this was not an easy idea for me to take in. I was just so used to calling God Lord and King and Father. And I was satisfied with these images, especially the triumphal ones which made me feel protected, secure. The idea of calling God Mother, Sister, Partner, Playmate, Friend – more relational images drawn from the experiences of women – that felt like heresy.

Also, to be honest, these new images challenged me to think of my relationship to God not just in terms of child to parent or loyal subject to mighty king. I was being invited to mature in my relationship, to see myself not just as a child needing protection but as a potential channel of Love, a way through which God could pour Her power and love into the world. These new images were inviting me to think in terms of partnership, collaboration. They were opening me to a radically new understanding of *God's* need for *me*. In my prayer I was being invited to offer God more of me, to become a sanctuary, a wellspring of living water where the Chosen One could be refreshed.

Before we go further, it's important to remember that God is neither male nor female; God is Spirit. Yet when we are told that only masculine words may be used to name God, it's hard not to think of "Him" as male. By using both male and female pronouns, referring to God as "She" as well as "He," as Mother as well as Father, we signal that God is neither one or the other but has characteristics of both. It helps us realize that, in the words of Johnson, "maternity is as much a part of God as majesty."

As I lived with this new learning over time, I began putting two and two together. Within myself and within many of the women I served, there was a startling lack of self-confidence, in spite of obvious gifts and accomplishments. Even after years of immersion in enlightened feminist teachings, I saw us looking toward men for protection and direction, as if they were somehow endowed with superior abilities, making them more capable of running things. Which isn't true. What they do have, says Jean Baker Miller in her beautiful little book, *Toward a New Psychology of Women*, is "more permission and more practice."

And as I thought about it, the men who came to my workshops would often admit to being weary of all the expectations placed on them to provide, protect, produce. Men aren't super people; they don't have all the answers; they often need help but may not know how to ask. Any show of vulnerability puts them at risk of ridicule.

I remember my former husband coming home after work one night with a story about a male colleague on his marketing team. Apparently the ad agency was showing the team a brand new ad, one with moving music and beautiful images of a world of peace and harmony. When the lights came up, the man had tears in his eyes. His colleagues laughed at him. "He'll never live that down," my husband said.

In their effort to appear all-powerful, to fulfill the demands of the cultural stereotype, men often push themselves beyond their limits, endangering their health and compromising their chance for a happy life. Underneath the façade, they are often scared and lonely. They may want closer connection but are reluctant to reach out for fear of appearing "needy."

Could there possibly be a correlation here between the struggles of these women to experience themselves as powerful, and these men to admit their vulnerability – and our images of God? Was this lopsided naming of God resulting not only in the diminishment of women's sense of self-worth and agency, but also in the inflation of men's sense of authority and responsibility?

Had I known God as Queen as well as King, as Mother as well as Father, as Sister as well as Savior, might it have allowed me to embrace myself more fully as a woman and value my ways of being as equally vital? Would it have heightened in me a sense of responsibility to bring my gifts to bear on the wider world? Instead of always "letting God do it"? In some ways was I complicit, preferring a lesser role because it kept me from exposure to the real risks of a front-line life?

Had men known God as Mother as well as Father, as Friend as well as King, would they have been more at ease with their vulnerability, more willing to express their emotional needs, more open to partnerships, less determined to win? My younger son, who was about fourteen when all this was stirring in me, expressed it well one day. After I finished making an elaborate ten-minute defense for my point of view, he said: "I get it. It's like for all these centuries we've been looking at God with only one eye." Out of the mouths of babes...

Shortly after the class ended, I was invited to give a talk in a local parish. I chose to talk about this subject, knowing it would likely have a mixed reception but hoping to stimulate some good conversation. Along with the talk I developed a slide show using images drawn from both men's and women's experience – God as Mother, Sister, Lover, Friend, Playmate... as well as Lord, King, Master, Messiah. One picture was of a young boy clasping his grandmother around the waist, his head buried in her ample belly. She was leaning over him, her arms resting lightly on his back. God as Grandmother.

After the show was over and the lights went up, no one spoke for a long time. Then one man, who had obviously been deeply moved, said, "That picture of the boy with his grandmother..." He stopped to collect himself. "If I had been raised with an image of God that looked like that, my whole life would have been different."

A woman in the audience came up afterwards to tell me that all her life she had been unable to pray to God as Father. Her own father had been abusive, and calling God Father had brought to mind images of cruelty. "Thank God I had Mary," she said.

As I end this piece, I want to thank you for walking with me through this treacherous terrain. It's difficult to imagine a radical change in our language for God. I know that. And yet, do we have a choice? What difference would it make to open our other eye, to see God through the lens of women's experience as well as men's? Perhaps it's time we found out.

Reflection Questions:

- What difference *would* it make to speak of God in female as well as male terms?

- How does this idea sit with you? Are you upset, confused, elated, at ease?

- How do you name the Divine now, and how has your naming changed?

Journal

Journal

15

MY LIFE IS A LISTENING

*"Create a clearing in the dense forest of your life
and wait there patiently, until the song that is your life
falls into your own cupped hands."*

~ Martha Postlewaite

I wrote the following piece fifteen years ago, for Richard
Rohr's *Radical Grace* magazine. I include it here because the
truth it bears has become more and more true for me as I
age. I now know beyond a shadow of a doubt that the key to a
joyful, fruitful life is learning to live in God, learning to trust
in God, and letting ourselves be led. Time spent quietly each
day, connecting with the wisdom within, allows us to make
choices that move us toward life. We learn, in Rohr's words,
to "trust the river...The river is flowing. We are in it. The river
is God's providential love – so do not be afraid."

I have always admired intentional people – people who
seemed to know where they were going and how to get there.

I've tried with some success to be that way myself – to make my life my project, to pick out my targets, focus my energy, go for the goal. I haven't always hit the mark, but by and large I've gotten where I wanted to go and I am satisfied.

Yet lately I've begun to notice a strange shift occurring in me, a call to do things differently, to loosen my grip, to let myself be led. It is not a comfortable feeling but one I know somehow to be right for me.

It is an invitation to trust, to believe – in the absence of any concrete proof – that maybe, just maybe, the best is yet to come, and yielding is the only way to get there.

Never mind that this goes against everything I ever learned, that it requires turning my back on the prevailing wisdom, which insists that the opposite of control is chaos and letting go is downright dangerous, because God knows what might happen.

Precisely!

I wrote this in my journal: "At fifty-five I am being invited to rethink the way I live my life, to open myself to the possibility that I have done all I can with the tools at hand. The things I crave most deeply – peace, joy, healing, wholeness – are within reach at last, but they will continue to elude me until I learn to live another way."

I know for one thing that I must learn to slow down, to be more quiet. I must not be so tied to being popular, successful, secure. I must start to cultivate the great virtues: charity, humility, trust, courage. I must learn to listen to what's going on inside of me; pay closer attention to the still, small voice that stirs when I stay still. I must be willing to step beyond what's comfortable, to open to an unbounded life. Listening will become vital to me now, the way quick reflexes are vital to a race car driver.

A while back I was flipping through a catalog, getting ready to throw it in the trash, when a picture caught my eye. It was of a woman sitting in a tree on a moonlit summer night, her knees drawn close to her body, her head resting against the tree trunk. She seemed alert, attentive, waiting. The caption underneath read: "My life is a listening."

The picture was no bigger than a postage stamp, and yet it captivated me. I cut it out and taped it in the front of my calendar where I would catch a glimpses of her as I flipped to my schedule for the day. My life is a listening...

During Lent this year I made a special effort to sit quietly with the Scriptures every morning, asking God to speak to me through these familiar words in a new way. One day I came across these lines from Isaiah, and felt a tug inside myself: "Do not remember the former things, or consider the things of old. I am about to do a new thing in you."

It was like a lens had been focused and a blurry image became clear. In that moment I knew I was being presented with a choice, one I was free to accept or to refuse. If I said no, life would go on much as before. If I said yes, I would be on the way to a new life – not all at once but little by little, day by day, I would be made new.

I was being drawn by Love into relationship. The invitation both thrills and frightens me. What will be required? What has to be left behind? And what...no...*Who* lies ahead?

In her book, *The Rising*, Wendy Wright speaks of what following God feels like: "If you think you sense the will of God in your life in some long-range highly detailed plan, something you can see stretching out with clear goals and successes in the future, that is not the will of God. If, however, you have an insistent sense that the next, very hesitant step beyond which you can see nothing is in fact the step that must be taken, that is most likely the will of God for you."

Isaiah, whose own life was one long surrender, echoes this when he gives this unflinching insight into the ways of God: "I will lead the blind on their journey, in a way that they know not. In unknown places I will guide them. I will turn darkness into light , and rough places into level ground."

For those of us who prefer to be in charge, to know beforehand what will be required of us, this is not good news. Even the reassurance that God goes before us isn't enough.

That doesn't change things. When we go with God there are no maps, no clear destination, no guarantees of success. We only know what we need to know, which is the next step. And as we take that step, and the next and the next, life mysteriously begins to open up. We learn to live by faith, and life gets deep and free.

The choice is always ours. God calls, then waits.

I linger at the border, assessing risks, mourning losses, testing the waters, stalling for time, thankful for the steadfast love that will never abandon me. The calendar on my wall reads May 8. I open my book of daily meditations and read this from the poet Ovid: "By yielding I may obtain victory."

Reflection Questions:

- What experiences have opened you to Love?
  Helped you trust God more?

- What experiences damaged trust and need healing
  so Love can flow freely?

- What do you need from God, from yourself,
  from your loved ones, your faith community to
  deepen your "Yes" to God's presence and action
  in your life?

- Stop. Be still. Listen.
  What do you hear?

Journal

_____

_____

_____

_____

_____

_____

_____

_____

_____

_____

_____

_____

_____

_____

_____

_____

_____

_____

_____

_____

_____

_____

Journal

Judith Krone

ACKNOWLEDGMENTS

I suppose there are writers among us who can simply sit down and write. Five hours a day, five days a week, and a year or two later, Voila! A book.

That's not me.

For years, I have talked about writing a book – as a way to share the wisdoms I had gained from years of walking with people on the spiritual journey. But somehow it never happened.

Every once in a while I would say to myself: "OK this is it!" I would block off time on my calendar; tell friends not to call before lunch. I'd clear off my desk, retrieve all folders from my file drawers labeled THE BOOK, take up pad and pen, and dive in. I would slosh around for a week or two, then look back at what I had done and promptly despair. I knew the answer was to push through, but since no one had me tied to the mast, I'd find excuses to slip away.

I wanted to write; I had things I wanted to say; but it was hard...and lonely...(sniff, sniff)...and who would want to read it anyway? Why couldn't I just let it go, satisfy myself with my day job: doing spiritual direction, conducting classes, giving retreats? Wasn't that enough?

I guess not. Like a feral cat, no matter how often I shooed it away, the desire wouldn't leave me alone. It began to feel like a call I couldn't ignore. So did I relent? Not yet. Instead I did what writers who don't write do: I read books on writing, listened to tapes on writing, went to writers' conferences and talked about writing. I even went once to a Memoir Writing workshop, and got mad at the instructor for spending too little time instructing and too much time making us write.

I wish I was exaggerating, but I'm not. This is all true.

I shared my distress with my friends. I talked to my therapist. I prayed to Frances de Sales, the patron saint of writers. I even paid visits to people I knew who wrote books and took copious notes on their processes.

It became a joke.

But my friends wouldn't laugh.

And that is the amazing thing about these people who are so dear to me. Not only did they not laugh at me; they kept telling me to keep at it. They didn't get impatient with the whining; they didn't roll their eyes at my latest plan. Every feeble effort – they were there to back me up.

Why? Perhaps because they knew something I didn't. They knew I wasn't lazy or crazy; I was afraid. They knew one day I'd do it, and that their job was simply to keep the faith.

And so at long last – by faith and by grace – I got over myself and got on with the work. Is it the Second Coming? Not quite. Just a collection of reflections on subjects dear to my heart. It's a thrill to be done, and to dedicate this little book to all of you who kept this little engine running until at last she did produce – Voila! A book.

"I call you by name..."
~ Isaiah 43

To Sr. Mary Dennison, pure presence, light on the water, shelter in the storm. To Sr. Marcie Anibas, who took me from the grave and sprinkled me with living water. To Sr. Mary Kay Finneran, who models for me courage, deep wisdom, and fierce charity. To Sr. Kathryn Cliatt, for her steadfast care in the worst of times, and for our treasured trailer talks. To Sr. Gracie Myerjack, for always knowing the way home. To Fay and Steve and Green Bough, for the light, the love, the laughter – and the peppermint patties.

To my sister Carola and my brother John, for who they are and how they love and for their stone strong faith in me. To Charlotte Keller, Kathleen O'Connor, and Jim Mengert, my pit crew. For the way we share our lives together. You light up my life and make me my best self. Not to mention the laughs! Special thanks to Charlotte, for telling me point blank: "You are a writer. Now go write!" And to Kathleen, who shared with me her experience, strength and hope – gifts of pure gold.

To Trisha Sinnott and Beverley Elliott, sisters, soulmates, three-in-one. To Nan Ross, for helping me know where the red birds are. To Beverly Key, for realizing what the black bird meant to me. To Dorothy Brooks, for never letting the saboteur get the upper hand, and for the magic beads-in-a-box. To Suzanne Carr, for her lifelong commitment to helping women live full lives. To beloved Sharon, for believing in this work.

To Chris Neilands and Barb Gifford and Beckie Bullard and Chris DiMuzio, my Chrysalis Center sisters, for showing up and circling me; for insisting that this work was mine to do, and I could do it. Extra special gratitude to Chris Neilands, whose artistry in coaching me made the crucial difference. Without her considerable skills and her determination to pull me through, this effort would have wound up in a heap with all the others. She, more than anyone else, helped birth this baby. Special thanks as well, to Laura Nalesnik, my designer, for handling my work so gently and dressing her so beautifully for publication.

To Tere Canzoneri, who has walked with me through

fire, frost, and flood, and never fails to lead me in right paths. To Pierre Ferrari, my former husband, for giving me a life that allowed me to follow the thread. To all the people with whom I have walked this great pilgrimage of life – in spiritual direction, in discernment circles, in book groups, on retreats. It has been good for me to share with you this walk, this work, this joy of waking up and waking up some more. You are all a part of me. This book belongs to you too.

Lastly, to my sons Peter and Oliver, who make me glad. There are no words to say what they have done for me.

Lalor and her two sons, Oliver and Peter Ferrari

About the Author

Lalor Cadley is founder and director of Chrysalis Center, an ecumenical Spirituality Center grounded in the Christian tradition. Opened in 1995, the Center offers spiritual direction, discernment circles, book studies, and retreats designed to promote attentiveness to the stirrings of the Holy within and among us.

Lalor received her certification in spiritual direction from the Spiritual Direction Institute in Houston, Texas. She holds a Masters degree from Regis University in Denver, Colorado, in Adult Spiritual Formation. Her columns on the spiritual life have appeared in the Atlanta Journal Constitution. She is also an Associate of Green Bough House of Prayer in Adrian, GA.

Lalor has two grown sons and lives in Atlanta.

To contact Lalor, please visit her Website:
www.lalorcadley.com